ISBN 978-1-331-41906-8
PIBN 10187497

This book is a reproduction of an important historical work. Forgotten Books uses
state-of-the-art technology to digitally reconstruct the work, preserving the original format
whilst repairing imperfections present in the aged copy. In rare cases, an imperfection in
the original, such as a blemish or missing page, may be replicated in our edition. We do,
however, repair the vast majority of imperfections successfully; any imperfections that
remain are intentionally left to preserve the state of such historical works.

1 MONTH OF
FREE
READING

at

www.ForgottenBooks.com

By purchasing this book you are
eligible for one month membership to
ForgottenBooks.com, giving you
unlimited access to our entire
collection of over 700,000 titles via
our web site and mobile apps.

To claim your free month visit:

www.forgottenbooks.com/free187497

PRINCE ALBERT'S

GOLDEN PRECEPTS:

OR,

THE OPINIONS AND MAXIMS

OF

HIS ROYAL HIGHNESS

THE PRINCE CONSORT.

SELECTED FROM HIS ADDRESSES, ETC.

SOME NOW FOR THE FIRST TIME COLLECTED, AND CAREFULLY ARRANGED.

WITH AN INDEX.

LONDON:
SAMPSON LOW, SON, AND CO.

47, LUDGATE HILL.

1862.

London: R. Clay, Son, and Taylor, Printers,
Bread Street Hill

PREFACE.

No attempt has hitherto been made to present in a convenient form the opinions of his Royal Highness the Prince Consort on the many important and interesting subjects with which his benevolent and active mind was unceasingly occupied. To the Society of Arts belongs the honour of having first published a collection of his public addresses, comprising, as stated in the preface, with one or two exceptions, those which bore on questions of social progress. This publication, however, necessarily contained much which was only of special application, or of a merely formal or temporary character, and having been published early in 1857, it comprises, of course, no speech delivered since that date.

The aim of the compiler of the present volume has been to collect from all the speeches and addresses delivered by his Royal Highness every passage which could stand alone, as embodying distinct thoughts, or reflections of general application, or which appeared interesting, as expressing an opinion or personal feeling of their illustrious author. His career was one rather of good deeds than many words. Its record will be best found in the ever-extending influences of his public labours; but if the occasions on which he clothed his ideas in language were few, his addresses abound in passages which Englishmen would not willingly let die. These have been carefully selected and arranged, without reference to the time at which they were spoken, with the view to give the volume, as far as the nature of the matter would allow, the varied character of a book of table-talk; and thus to present a faithful miniature of his mind.

CONTENTS.

Contents.

PRINCE ALBERT'S

GOLDEN PRECEPTS.

INTERESTS OF CLASSES IDENTICAL.

DEPEND upon it, the interests of classes too often contrasted are identical, and it is only ignorance which prevents their uniting for each other's advantage. To dispel that ignorance, to show how man can help man, notwithstanding the complicated state of civilized society, ought to be the aim of every philanthropic person; but it is more peculiarly the duty of those who, under the blessing of Divine Providence, enjoy station, wealth, and education.

B

Let them be careful, however, to avoid any dictatorial interference with labour and employment, which frightens away capital, destroys that freedom of thought and independence of action which must remain to every one if he is to work out his own happiness, and impairs that confidence under which alone engagements for mutual benefit are possible.

WISE BENEVOLENCE.

GOD has created man imperfect, and left him with many wants, as it were to stimulate each to individual exertion, and to make all feel that it is only by united exertions and combined action that these imperfections can be supplied, and these wants satisfied. This presupposes self-reliance and confidence in each other. To show the way how these individual exertions can be directed with the greatest benefit, and to foster that confidence upon which the readiness to assist each other depends, this Society* deems its most sacred duty.

There has been no ostentatious display of charity or munificence, nor the pretension of becoming the arbiter of the fate of thousands, but the quiet working out of particular schemes of social improvement ; for which, however, as I said before, the Society has only established examples for the community at large to follow.

THE SLAVE TRADE.

I have been induced to preside at this meeting,† from a conviction of its paramount importance to the great interests of humanity and justice. I deeply regret that the benevolent and persevering

* From a speech at a Meeting of the Servants' Provident and Benevolent Society.

† The brief remarks in this paragraph derive a peculiar interest from the fact of their forming the first public address of Prince Albert in this country. They were spoken at a meeting of the Society for the Extinction of the Slave Trade, held in London, on the 1st of June, 1840.

exertions of England to abolish that atrocious traffic in human beings, at once the desolation of Africa and the blackest stain upon civilized Europe, have not as yet led to any satisfactory conclusion. I sincerely trust that this great country will not relax in its efforts until it has finally and for ever put an end to a state of things so repugnant to the spirit of Christianity, and to the best feelings of our nature.

SCIENCE AND COMMON SENSE.

It is sometimes objected by the ignorant that science is uncertain and changeable, and they point with a malicious kind of pleasure to the many exploded theories which have been superseded by others, as a proof that the present knowledge may be also unsound, and, after all, not worth having. But they are not aware that, while they think to cast blame upon science, they bestow, in fact, the highest praise upon her.

For this is precisely the difference between science and prejudice: that the latter keeps stubbornly to its position, whether disproved or not, whilst the former is an unarrestable movement towards the fountain of truth, caring little for cherished authorities or sentiments, but continually progressing; feeling no false shame at her shortcomings, but, on the contrary, the highest pleasure, when freed from an error, at having advanced another step towards the attainment of divine truth—a pleasure not even intelligible to the pride of ignorance.

We also hear, not unfrequently, science and practice, scientific knowledge and common sense, contrasted as antagonistic. A strange error! for science is eminently practical, and must be so, as she sees and knows what she is doing, whilst mere common practice is condemned to work in the dark, applying natural ingenuity to unknown powers to obtain a known result.

THE DUTY OF THE RICH.

OUR Heavenly Father, in His boundless goodness, has made His creatures that they should be
happy, and in His wisdom has fitted His means
to his ends, giving to all of them different qualities and faculties, in using and developing which
they fulfil their destiny, and, running their uniform
course according to his prescription, they find that
happiness which He has intended for them.   Man
alone is born into this world with faculties far
nobler than the other creatures, reflecting the
image of Him who has willed that there should
be beings on earth to know and worship Him, but
endowed with the power of self-determination,
having reason given him for his guide.   He can
develop his faculties, place himself in harmony with
his Divine prototype, and attain that happiness
which is offered to him on earth, to be completed

hereafter in entire union with Him through the mercy of Christ. But he can also leave these faculties unimproved, and miss his mission on earth. He will then sink to the level of the lower animals, forfeit happiness, and separate from his God, whom he did not know how to find. I say man has no right to do this—he has no right to throw off the task which is laid upon him for his happiness; it is his duty to fulfil his mission to the utmost of his power; but it is our duty, the duty of those whom Providence has removed from this awful struggle and placed beyond this fearful danger, manfully, unceasingly, and untiringly to aid by advice, assistance, and example, the great bulk of the people, who, without such aid, must almost inevitably succumb to the difficulty of their task. They will not cast from them the aiding hand, and the Almighty will bless the labours of those who work in His cause.

THE REAL MAGIC WAND.

No human pursuits make any material progress until science is brought to bear upon them. We have seen, accordingly, many of them slumber for centuries upon centuries; but from the moment that science has touched them with her magic wand, they have sprung forward and taken strides which amaze and almost awe the beholder.

Look at the transformation which has gone on around us since the laws of gravitation, electricity, magnetism, and the expansive power of heat have become known to us. It has altered our whole state of existence—one might say, the whole face of the globe. We owe this to science, and to science alone; and she has other treasures in store for us, if we will but call her to our assistance.

DETERMINATION TO AVOID POLITICAL PARTIES.

I REMEMBER well with what regret, when, shortly after I came of age, the Companies of the Goldsmiths and of the Fishmongers offered me their freedom, I found myself compelled to decline this honour, being informed that, identified as they were by historical tradition, and still representing two opposite political parties, I could make a choice only of one of them, and fully sensible that, like the Sovereign to whom I had just been united, and to devote my whole existence to whom it had become my privilege, I could belong only to the nation at large, free from the trammels and above the dissensions of political parties.

I well remember, too, how much pleased I was when the two Companies, waiving some of their statutes, finally agreed both to receive me amongst them.

IMPROVEMENT OF THE LABOURING CLASS.

WHEN the Society for the Improvement of the Condition of the Labouring Classes was first established on its present footing, I accepted with great pleasure the offer of becoming its President.

I saw in this offer a proof of appreciation of my feelings of sympathy and interest for that class of our community which has most of the toil, and least of the enjoyments, of this world. I conceived that great advantage would accrue from the endeavours of influential persons, who were wholly disinterested, to act the part of a friend to those who required that advice and assistance, which none but a friend could tender with advantage.

This Society has always held this object before its eyes, and has been labouring in that direction. You are all aware that it has established model lodging-houses, loan-funds, and the system of allotments of ground in different parts of the country;

but it has been careful only to establish examples and models, mindful that any real improvement which was to take place must be the result of the exertions of the working-people themselves.

————

MAN A DIVINE INSTRUMENT.

Whilst formerly the great mental energies strove at universal knowledge, and that knowledge was confined to the few, now they are directed on specialities, and in these, again, even to the minutest points; but the knowledge acquired becomes at once the property of the community at large; for, whilst formerly discovery was wrapped in secrecy, the publicity of the present day causes that, no sooner is a discovery or invention made than it is already improved upon and surpassed by competing efforts. The products of all quarters of the globe are placed at our disposal, and we have only to choose which is the best and the cheapest for our purposes, and the powers of production are entrusted to the stimulus of *competition and capital.*

So man is approaching a more complete fulfilment of that great and sacred mission which he has to perform in this world. His reason being created after the image of God, he has to use it to discover the laws by which the Almighty governs His creation, and by making these laws his standard of action, to conquer nature to his use; himself a Divine instrument.

Science discovers these laws of power, motion, and transformation; industry applies them to the raw matter, which the earth yields us in abundance, but which becomes valuable only by knowledge. Art teaches us the immutable laws of beauty and symmetry, and gives to our productions forms in accordance to them.

CHARACTER OF THE LATE SIR ROBERT PEEL.

THERE is but one alloy to my feelings of satisfaction and pleasure in seeing you here assembled again,* and that is, the painful remembrance that one is missing from amongst us who felt so warm an interest in our scheme† and took so active a part in promoting its success, the last act of whose public life was attending at the Royal Commission: my admiration for whose talents and character, and gratitude for whose devotion to the Queen, and private friendship towards myself, I feel a consolation in having this public opportunity to express.

Only at our last meeting we were still admiring his eloquence and the earnestness with which he appealed to you to uphold, by your exertions and personal sacrifices, what was to him the highest

* From a speech at a banquet given by the Lord Mayor of York, October 25, 1850.

† The Great Exhibition.

object—the honour of his country; he met you the following day together with other commissioners, to confer with you upon the details of our undertaking : and you must have been struck, as everybody has been who has had the benefit of his advice upon practical points, with the attention, care, and sagacity with which he treated the minutest details, proving that to a great mind nothing is little, from the knowledge that in the moral and intellectual, as in the physical world, the smallest point is only a link in that great chain, and holds its appointed place in that great whole, which is governed by the Divine Wisdom.

The constitution of Sir Robert Peel's mind was peculiarly that of a statesman, and of an English statesman : he was liberal from feeling, but conservative upon principle. Whilst his impulse drove him to foster progress, his sagacious mind and great experience showed him how easily the whole machinery of a state and of society is deranged, and how important, but how difficult also, it is to direct its further development in accordance with its fundamental principles, like organic growth in nature. It was peculiar to him, that in great things, as in small, all the difficulties and objections occurred to him at first; he would anxiously consider them, pause, and warn against rash resolutions; but having convinced himself, after a long and careful investigation, that a step was not only right to be taken, but of the practical mode also of safely taking it, it became to him a necessity and a duty to take it: all his caution and apparent timidity changed into courage and power of action, and at the same time readiness cheerfully to make any personal sacrifice which its execution might demand.

If he has had so great an influence over this country, it was from the nation recognising in his qualities the true type of the English character, which is essentially practical. Warmly attached to his institutions, and revering the bequests left to him by the industry, wisdom, and piety of his forefathers, the Englishman attaches little value to any theoretical scheme. It will attract his attention only after having been for some time

placed before him ; it must have been thoroughly
investigated and discussed before he will entertain
it. Should it be an empty theory, it will fall to
the ground during this time of probation ; should
it survive this trial, it will be on account of the
practical qualities contained in it; but its adoption
in the end will entirely depend upon its har-
monizing with the national feeling, the historic
development of the country, and the peculiar
nature of its institutions.

It is owing to these national qualities that
England, whilst constantly progressing, has still
preserved the integrity of her constitution from
the earliest times, and has been protected from
wild schemes whose chief charm lies in their
novelty, whilst around us we have seen unfortu-
nately whole nations distracted, and the very fabric
of society endangered, from the levity with which
the result of the experience of generations, the
growth of ages, has been thrown away to give
place to temporarily favourite ideas.

SUPPOSED CERTAINTIES, ONLY PROBABILITIES.

OUR statistical science does not even say that this must be so ; it only states that it has been so, and leaves it to the naturalist or political economist to argue that it is probable, from the number of times in which it has been found to be so, that it will be so again as long as the same causes are operating. It thus gave birth to that part of mathematical science called the calculus of probabilities, and even established the theory that in the natural world there exist no certainties at all, but only probabilities. Although this doctrine, destroying man's feeling of security to a certain extent, has startled and troubled some, it is no less true that, while we may reckon with a thoughtless security on the sun rising to-morrow, this is only a probable event, the probability of which is capable of being expressed by a determined mathematical fraction. From the vast collection of existing statistical facts, the probable

duration of man's life has been established with
such precision, that our insurance offices are able
to enter with each individual into a precise bar-
gain on the value of his life; and yet this does
not imply an impious pretension to determine
when this individual is really to die.

———————

PROGRESS OF AGRICULTURE.

AGRICULTURE, which was once the main pursuit
of this as of every other nation, holds even now,
notwithstanding the development of commerce
and manufactures, a fundamental position in the
realm; and, although time has changed the position which the owner of the land, with his feudal
dependants, held in the empire, the country
gentleman with his wife and children, the country
clergyman, the tenant, and the labourer, still form
a great, and I hope united family, in which we
gladly recognise the foundation of our social
state.

Science and mechanical improvement have in these days changed the mere practice of cultivating the soil into an industrial pursuit, requiring capital, machinery, industry, and skill, and perseverance in the struggle of competition. This is another great change, but we must consider it a great progress, as it demands higher efforts and a higher intelligence.

———

MISSIONARY LABOURS.

WE are not commemorating an isolated fact* which may have been glorious or useful to the country, but we are thankfully acknowledging the Divine favour which has attended exertions which have been unremitting during the lapse of one hundred and fifty years. We are met at the same time to invoke the further continuance of that favour, pledging ourselves not to relax in

* From a speech at the third jubilee of the "Society for the Propagation of the Gospel in Foreign Parts."

our efforts to extend to those of our brethren who are settled in distant lands, and building up communities and states where man's footsteps had first to be imprinted on the soil, and wild nature yet to be conquered to his use, those blessings of Christianity which form the foundation of our community and of our state.

This Society was first chartered by that great man, William the Third, the greatest sovereign this country has to boast of; by whose sagacity and energy was closed that bloody struggle for civil and religious liberty which so long had convulsed this country, and who secured to us the inestimable advantages of our constitution, and of our Protestant faith.

Having thus placed the country upon a safe basis at home, he could boldly meet her foes abroad, and contribute to the foundation of that colonial empire which forms so important a part of our present greatness; and honour be to him for his endeavour to place this foundation upon the rock of the Church.

The first jubilee of the Society fell in times

when religious apathy had succeeded to the over-excitement of the preceding age. Lax morals and a sceptical philosophy began to undermine the Christian faith, treating with indifference and even ridicule the most sacred objects. Still this Society persevered in its labours with unremitting zeal, turning its chief attention to the North American continent, where a young and vigorous society was rapidly growing into a people.

The second jubilee found this country in a most critical position : she had obtained, by the peace of Amiens, a moment's respite from the tremendous contest in which she had been en-gaged with her continental rival, and which she had soon to renew, in order to maintain her own existence, and to secure a permanent peace to Europe. Since the last jubilee, the American colonies, which had originally been peopled chiefly by British subjects who had left their homes to escape the yoke of religious intole-rance and oppression, had thrown off their allegiance to the mother country in defence of civil rights, the attachment to which they had

carried with them from the British soil. Yet
this Society was not dismayed, but in a truly
Christian spirit continued its labours in the
neighbouring North American and West Indian
settlements.

This, the third jubilee, falls in a happier epoch,
when peace is established in Europe, and religious
fervour is rekindled, and at an auspicious moment when we are celebrating a festival of the
civilization of mankind, to which all quarters of
the globe have contributed their productions, and
are sending their people, for the first time recognising their advancement as a common good,
their interests as identical, their mission on
earth the same.

And this civilization rests on Christianity, could
only be raised on Christianity, can only be main-
tained by Christianity! the blessings of which
are now carried by this Society to the vast
territories of India and Australasia, which last are
again to be peopled by the Anglo-Saxon race.

THE LIMITS OF STATISTICS.

STATISTICAL science is comparatively new in its position among the sciences in general, and we must look for the cause of this tardy recognition to the fact, that it has the appearance of an incomplete science, and of being rather a helpmate to other sciences than having a right to claim that title for itself. But this is an appearance only; for if pure statistics, as a science, abstains from participating in the last and highest aim of all science, viz. the discovery and expounding the general laws which govern the universe, and leaves this duty to its more favoured sisters, the natural and the political sciences, this is done with conscious self-abnegation, for the purpose of protecting the purity and simplicity of its sacred task—the accumulation and verification of facts, unbiassed by any consideration of the ulterior use which may or can be made of them. Those general laws, therefore, in the knowledge of which we recognise one of the highest treasures of man on earth, are often unexpressed, though rendered self-apparent, as they may be read in the uncompromising rigid figures placed before him. It is difficult to see how, under such circumstances, and notwithstanding this self-imposed abnegation, statistical science, as such, should be subject to prejudice, reproach, and attack ; and yet the fact cannot be denied.

A FUTURE HAVEN OF COMMERCE.*

WE have been laying the foundation not only of a dock, as a place of refuge, safety, and refitment for mercantile shipping, and calculated even to receive the largest steamers in Her Majesty's navy, but it may be, and I hope it will be, the foundation of a great commercial port, destined in after times, when we shall long have quitted this scene, and when our names even may be for-

* From the speech on laying the first stone of the Docks at Great Grimsby, April 18, 1849.

gotten, to form another centre of life to the vast
and ever increasing commerce of the world, and
an important link in the connexion of the East
and the West. Nay, if I contemplate the extra-
ordinary rapidity of development which charac-
terises the undertakings of this age, it may not
even be too much to expect that some of us may
yet live to see this prospect in part realized.

THE BRITISH ASSOCIATION.

ONE of the latest undertakings of the Association has been, in conjunction with the Royal
Society, to attempt the compilation of a classified
Catalogue of Scientific Memoirs, which, by combining under one head the titles of all memoirs
written on a certain subject, will, when completed,
enable the student who wishes to gain information
on that subject to do so with the greatest ease.
It gives him as it were the plan of the house, and
the key to the different apartments in which the
treasures relating to his subject are stored, saving

him at once a painful and laborious search, and affording him at the same time an assurance that what is here offered contains the whole of the treasures yet acquired.

While this has been one of its latest attempts, the Association has from its very beginning kept in view that its main sphere of usefulness lay in that concentrated attention to all scientific opera- tions which a general gives to the movements of his army, watching and regulating the progress of his impetuous soldiers in the different directions to which their ardour may have led them, care- fully noting the gaps which may arise from their independent and eccentric action, and attentively observing what impediments may have stopped, or may threaten to stop, the progress of certain columns.

Thus it attempts to fix and record the position and progress of the different labours by its Reports on the state of Sciences published annually in its *Transactions:*—thus it directs the attention of the labourers to those gaps which require to be filled up, if the progress is to be a safe and steady one ;—thus it comes forward with a helping hand in striving to remove these impediments which the unaided efforts of the individual labourer have been or may be unable to overcome.

This is the twenty-ninth anniversary of the foundation of this Association ;* and well may we look back with satisfaction to its operation and achievements throughout the time of its existence. When, on the 27th of September, 1831, the meeting of the Yorkshire Philosophical Society took place at York, in the theatre of the Yorkshire Museum, under the presidency of the late Earl Fitzwilliam, then Viscount Milton, and the Rev. W. Vernon Harcourt eloquently set forth the plan for the formation of a British Association for the - Promotion of Science, which he showed to have become a want for his country, the most ardent supporter of this resolution could not have anticipated that it would start into life full-grown, as it were ; enter at once upon its career of usefulness, and pursue it without deviation from the original design, triumphing over the oppositions

* 27th September, 1859.

which it had to encounter, in common with every-thing that is new and claims to be useful. This proved that the want was a real, and not an imaginary one, and that the mode in which it was intended to supply that want was based upon a just appreciation of unalterable truths.

LANDLORDS AND THEIR TENANTS.

THIS visit * has brought me for the first time to the county of Lincoln, so celebrated for its agricultural pursuits, and showing a fine example of the energy of the national character, which has, by dint of perseverance, succeeded in trans-forming unhealthy swamps into the richest and most fertile soil in the kingdom. I could not have witnessed finer specimens of Lincolnshire farming, than have been shown to me on his estates by my noble host,† who has made me acquainted not only with the agricultural improve-ments which are going on amongst you, but with

* To Great Grimsby, April 18, 1849.
† The Earl of Yarborough.

that most gratifying state of the relation between Landlord and Tenant which exists here, and which I hope may become an example, in time to be followed throughout the country. Here it is that the real advantage and the prosperity of both do not depend upon the written letter of agreements, but on that mutual trust and confidence which has in this country for a long time been held a sufficient security to both, to warrant the extensive outlay of capital, and the engagement in farming operations on the largest scale.

FEATURES OF ENGLISH CHARACTER.

THIS work * has been undertaken, like almost all the national enterprises of this great country, by *private* exertion, with *private* capital, and at *private* risk; and it shares with them likewise that other feature so peculiar to the enterprises of Englishmen, that strongly attached as they are to the institutions of their country, and gratefully

* The *Great Grimsby Docks.*

acknowledging the protection of those laws under which their enterprises are undertaken and flourish, they love to connect them, in some manner, directly with the authority of the Crown, and the person of the Sovereign ; and it is the appreciation of this circumstance which has impelled me at once to respond to your call, as the readiest mode of testifying to you how strongly Her Majesty the Queen values and reciprocates this feeling.

THE METHOD OF LORD BACON.

THE British Association embraces in its sphere of action, if not the whole range of the sciences, yet a very large and important section of them, those known as the *inductive sciences*, excluding all that are not approached by the inductive method of investigation. It has, for instance (and considering its peculiar organization and mode of action, perhaps not unwisely), eliminated from its consideration and discussions those which come under the description of moral and political sciences. This has not been done from undervaluing their importance, and denying their sacred right to the special attention of mankind, but from a desire to deal with those subjects only which can be reduced to positive proof, and do not rest on opinion or faith. The subjects of the moral and political sciences involve not only opinions, but feelings; and their discussion frequently rouses passions. For feelings are "subjective," as the German metaphysician has it—they are inseparable from the individual being—an attack upon them is felt as one upon the person itself; whilst facts are "objective" and belong to everybody— they remain the same facts at all times and under all circumstances : they can be proved; they have to be proved, and when proved, are finally settled. It is with facts only that the Association deals. There may for a time exist differences of opinion on these also, but the process of removing them and resolving them into agreement is a different one from that in the moral and political sciences. These are generally approached by the *deductive* process; but if the reasoning be ever so acute and logically correct, and the point of departure, which may be arbitrarily selected, is disputed, no agreement is possible; whilst we proceed here by the *inductive* process, taking nothing on trust, nothing for granted, but reasoning upwards from the meanest fact established, and making every step sure before going one beyond it, like the engineer in his approaches to a fortress. We thus gain ultimately a roadway, a ladder by which even a child may, almost without knowing it, ascend to the summit of truth, and obtain that immensely wide and extensive view which is spread below the feet of the astonished beholder. This road has been shown us by the great Bacon; and who can contemplate the prospects which it opens without almost falling into a trance similar to that in which he allowed his imagination to wander over future ages of discovery!

POSITION OF DOMESTIC SERVANTS.

WHO would not feel the deepest interest in the welfare of their Domestic Servants? Whose heart would fail to sympathise with those who minister to us in all the wants of daily life, attend us in sickness, receive us upon our first appearance in this world, and even extend their care to our mortal remains—who live under our roof, form our household, and are a part of our family?

And yet upon inquiry we find that in this metropolis the greater part of the inmates of the workhouse were domestic servants.

I am sure that this startling fact is no proof either of a want of kindness and liberality in masters towards their servants, or of vice in the latter, but is the natural consequence of that peculiar position in which the domestic servant is placed, passing periods during his life, in which he shares in the luxuries of an opulent master, and others in which he has not even the means of earning sufficient to sustain him through the day.

It is the consideration of these peculiar vicissitudes which makes it the duty of both master and servants to endeavour to discover and to agree upon some means for carrying the servant through life, safe from the temptations of the prosperous, and from the sufferings of the evil day.

THE USE AND ABUSE OF FIGURES.

THE public generally connect in their minds Statistics, if not with unwelcome taxation (for which they naturally form an important basis), certainly with political controversies, in which they are in the habit of seeing public men making use of the most opposite statistical results with equal assurance in support of the most opposite arguments. A great and distinguished French minister and statesman is even quoted as having boasted of the invention of what he is said to have called " l'art de grouper les chiffres ;" but if the same ingenuity and enthusiasm which may have suggested to him this art should have tempted him or others, as historians, to group facts also, it would be no more reasonable to make the historical facts answerable for the use made of them than it would be to make statistical science responsible for many an ingenious financial statement.   Yet this science has suffered materially in public estimation by such use, although the very fact that statesmen, financiers, physicians, and naturalists seek to support their statements and doctrines by statistics, shows conclusively that they all acknowledge them as the foundation of truth ; and this ought, therefore, to raise, instead of depressing, the science in the general esteem of the public.

OUR OBLIGATIONS TO THE PAST.

SCIENCE is not of yesterday. We stand on the shoulders of past ages, and the amount of observations made, and facts ascertained, has been transmitted to us and carefully preserved in the various storehouses of Science. Other crops have been reaped, but still lie scattered on the field. Many a rich harvest is ripe for cutting, but waits for the reaper. Economy of labour is the essence of good husbandry, and no less so in the field of Science.

NECESSITY OF METHOD.

Even the comparison of the same facts in different localities does not give us all the necessary materials from which to draw our conclusions; for we require, as much as anything else, the collection of observations of the same classes of facts in the same localities and under the same conditions, but at different times. It is only the elements of time, in the last instance, which enable us to test progress or regress— that is to say, life. Thus the physician, by feeling the pulse of the greatest number of persons coming under his observation, old and young, male and female, and at all seasons, arrives at the average number of the pulsations of the heart in man's normal condition; by feeling the pulse of the same person under the most varied circumstances and conditions, he arrives at a conclusion on this person s pulse; again, by feeling the pulse of the greatest variety of persons suffering from the same disease, he ascertains the general condition of the pulse under the influence of that disease; it is now only that, feeling a particular patient's pulse, he will be able to judge whether this person is afflicted by this peculiar disease, as far as that can be ascertained by its influence on the pulse.

But all these comparisons of the different classes of facts under different local conditions, and at different times, of which I have been speaking, depend not only as to their usefulness and as to the ease with which they can be undertaken, but even as to the possibility of undertaking them at all, on the similarity, nay congruity, of the method employed, and the expressions, figures, and conditions selected, under which the observations have been taken. Does not, then, the world at large owe the deepest obligations to a congress such as the one I am addressing, which has made it its especial task to produce this assimilation, and to place at the command of man the accumulated experience upon his own condition, scientifically elaborated and reduced in a manner to enable the meanest intellect to draw safe conclusions?

AN OLD CITY COMPANY.

ANYBODY may indeed feel proud to be enrolled a member of a Company which can boast of uninterrupted usefulness and beneficence during four centuries,* and holds to this day the same honourable position in the estimation of the country, which it did in the time of its first formation, although the progress of civilization and wealth has so vastly raised the community around it, exemplifying the possibility, in this happy country, of combining the general progress of mankind with a due reverence for the institutions, and even forms, which have been bequeathed to us by the piety and wisdom of our forefathers.

* The Merchant Taylors' Company, to which this refers, was first incorporated in 1466.

THE PHILOSOPHER AND THE CHILD.

THE labours of the man of science are at once the most humble and the loftiest which man can undertake. He only does what every little child does from its first awakening into life, and must do every moment of its existence; and yet he aims at the gradual approximation to divine truth itself. If, then, there exists no difference between the work of the man of Science and that of the merest child, what constitutes the distinction? Merely the conscious self-determination. The child observes what accident brings before it, and unconsciously forms its notion of it; the so-called practical man observes what his special work forces upon him, and he forms his notions upon it with reference to this particular work. The man of Science observes what he intends to observe, and knows why he intends it. The value which the peculiar object has in his eyes is not determined by accident, nor by an external cause, such as the mere connexion with work to be performed, but by the place which he knows this object to hold in the general universe of knowledge, by the relation which it bears to other parts of that general knowledge.

THE ROYAL ACADEMY.

HERE young artists are educated and taught the mysteries of their profession; those who have distinguished themselves and given proof of their talent and power receive a badge of acknowledgment from their professional brethren by being elected Associates of the Academy, and are at last, after long toil and continued exertion, received into a select aristocracy of a limited number, and shielded in any further struggle by their well-established reputation, of which the letters R. A. attached to their names give a pledge to the public.

If this body is often assailed from without, it shares only the fate of every aristocracy; if more than another, this only proves that it is even more difficult to sustain an aristocracy of merit than one of birth or of wealth, and may serve as a useful check upon yourselves when tempted at your elections to let personal predilections compete with real merit.

On one thing, however, you may rest assured, and that is the continued favour of the Crown. The same feelings which actuated George the Third in founding this institution still actuate the Crown in continuing to it its patronage and support, recognising in you a constitutional link, as it were, between the Crown itself and the artistic body. And when I look at the assemblage of guests at this table,* I may infer that the Crown does not stand alone in this respect, but that our feelings are shared also by the great and noble in the land.

* Spoken at the anniversary dinner in 1851.

IMPORTANCE OF CLASSIFYING KNOWLEDGE.

To arrange and classify that universe of knowledge becomes therefore the first, and perhaps the most important, object and duty of science. It is only when brought into a system, by separating the incongruous and combining those elements in which we have been enabled to discover the internal connexion which the Almighty has implanted in them, that we can hope to grapple with the boundlessness of His creation, and with the laws which govern both mind and matter.

FOREIGN DISTRUST OF THE GREAT EXHIBITION.

Although we perceive, in some countries, a fear that the advantages to be derived from the Exhibition will be mainly reaped by England, and a consequent distrust in the effects of our scheme upon their own interests, we must at the same time freely and gratefully acknowledge that our invitation has been received by all nations, with whom communication was possible, in that spirit of liberality and friendship in which it was tendered, and that they are making great exertions and incurring great expenses in order to meet our plans.

Of our own doings at the commission, I should have preferred to remain silent : but I cannot let this opportunity pass without telling you how much benefit we have derived, in our difficult labours, from your uninterrupted confidence in the intentions, at least, which guided our decisions; and that there has been no difference of opinion on any one subject, between us and the different local committees, which has not, upon personal consultation, and after open explanation and discussion, vanished, and given way to agreement and identity of purpose.*

Spoken at the banquet given by the Lord Mayor of York, Oct. 25, 1850.

A MODEL LODGING HOUSE.

I FEEL convinced that its existence will by degrees cause a complete change in the domestic comforts of the labouring classes, as it will exhibit to them that with real economy can bé combined advantages with which few of them have hitherto been acquainted ; whilst it will show to those who possess capital to invest, that they may do so with great profit and advantage to themselves, at the same time that they are dispensing those comforts to which I have alluded to their poorer brethren.

CHARACTERISTICS OF THE AGE.

I CONCEIVE it to be the duty of every educated person closely to watch and study the time in which he lives, and, as far as in him lies, to add his humble mite of individual exertion to further the accomplishment of what he believes Providence to have ordained.

Nobody, however, who has paid any attention to the peculiar features of our present era, will doubt for a moment that we are living at a period of most wonderful transition, which tends rapidly to accomplish that great end to which, indeed, all history points—*the realization of the unity of mankind.* Not a unity which breaks down the limits and levels the peculiar characteristics of the different nations of the earth, but rather a unity, the *result and ¿product* of those very national varieties and antagonistic qualities.

The distances which separated the different nations and parts of the globe are rapidly vanishing before the achievements of modern invention, and we can traverse them with incredible ease ; the languages of all nations are known, and their acquirement placed within the reach of everybody; thought is communicated with the rapidity, and even by the power, of lightning. On the other hand, the *great ¿principle of division of labour,* which may be called the moving power of civilization, is being extended to all branches of science, industry, and art.

MENDELSSOHN.

THE great master who, through the whole maze of his creation, from the soft whispering to the mighty raging of the elements, makes us conscious of the unity of his conception.

DEFECTS OF OUR CENSUS

THE official statistics of all countries have been improved, and, in regard to the census, the recommendations of the Brussels meeting have been generally carried out in a majority of states. I am sorry to have to admit the existence of some striking exceptions in England in this respect; for instance, the census of Great Britain and Ireland was not taken on precisely the same plan in essential particulars, thereby diminishing its value for general purposes. The judicial statistics ôf England and Wales do not show a complete comparative view of the operation of our judicial establishments ; nor, while we are in all the departments of the State most actively engaged in the preparation of valuable statistics, can we deny certain defects in our returns, which must be traced to the want of such a central

by the Congress at Brussels and Paris, to direct on a general plan all the great statistical operations to be prepared by the various departments. Such a commission would be most useful in preparing an annual digest of the statistics of the United Kingdom, of our widely scattered colonies, and of our vast Indian Empire. From such a digest the most important results could not fail to be elicited. One of the most useful results of the labours of the Congress has been the common agreement of all states to inquire into the causes of every death, and to return the deaths from the same causes under synonymous names, sanctioned by the Congress. It has in this instance set the example of establishing what is most desirable in all other branches of statistics, namely, the agreement upon well-defined terms.   There ought to exist no greater difficulty in arriving at such an agreement in the case of the various crimes than in that of " causes of death ; " and it must be remembered that it is one of the first tasks and duties of every science to start with a definition of terms.   What is it that is meant by a house, a family, an adult, an educated or an uneducated person, by murder, manslaughter, and so on?   It is evident that as long as a different sense is attached to these terms in different returns their use for comparison is *nil,* and for simple study very much deteriorated ; and still we have not yet arrived at such a simple and obvious desideratum !   The different weights, measures, and currencies, in which different statistics are expressed, cause further difficulties and impediments

POLITICAL ECONOMY.

FROM amongst the political sciences it has been the custom in modern times to detach one which admits of being severed from individual opinions, and of being reduced to abstract laws, derived from well-authenticated facts. I mean Political Economy, based on general statistics. A new Association has recently been formed, striving to comprehend in its investigations and discussions even a still more extended range of subjects, in what is called "Social Science." These efforts deserve our warmest approbation and goodwill. May they succeed in obtaining a purely and strictly scientific character! Our own Association has, since its meeting at Dublin, recognised the growing claims of political economy to scientific brotherhood, and admitted it into its statistical section. It could not have done so under abler guidance and happier auspices than the presidency of the Archbishop of Dublin, Dr. Whately, whose efforts in this direc-

E

tion are so universally appreciated. But even in this section, and while statistics alone were treated in it, the Association, as far back as 1833, made it a rule that, in order to insure positive results, only those classes of facts should be admitted which were capable of being expressed by numbers, and which promised, when sufficiently multiplied, to indicate general laws.

If, then, the main object of inductive science is the discovery of the laws which govern natural phenomena, the primary condition for its success is—accurate observation and collection of facts in such comprehensiveness and completeness as to furnish the philosopher with the necessary material from which to draw safe conclusions.

"CHARACTERS" TO SERVANTS.

ANY one who is acquainted with the annoyances and inconveniences connected with the present system of "characters to servants," will at once see the importance of the introduction

of a system by which the servant will be protected from that ruin which the caprice of a
single master (with whom he may even have
lived for a short time only) may inflict upon him,
and the master from the risk to which a character wrung from a former weak master by the im-
portunities of an undeserving servant, may expose
him.* Nor is it a small benefit to be conferred
upon a servant, to enable him, by appealing to
a long record of former services, to redeem
the disqualification which a single fault might
bring upon him.

Should we only succeed in inducing the public
at large to consider all these points, we shall have
the satisfaction of having furthered the interests
of a class which we find recorded, in the Report
of the last Census, as the most numerous in the
British population.

* Referring to a registry for servants.

FEELINGS ON PRESIDING AT A GREAT SCIENTIFIC ASSEMBLY.*

THE high position which science occupies, the vast number of distinguished men who labour in her sacred cause, and whose achievements, while spreading innumerable benefits, justly attract the admiration of mankind, contrasted strongly in my mind with the consciousness of my own insignificance in this respect. I, a simple ad mirer and would-be student of science, to take the place of the chief and spokesman of the scientific men of the day, assembled in furtherance of their important objects!—the thing appeared to me impossible. Yet, on reflection, I came to the conclusion that, if not as a contributor to, or director of your labours, I might still be useful to you, useful to science, by accepting your offer. Remembering that this Association is a popular Association, not a secret confraternity of men

* The meeting of the British Association at Aberdeen September, 1859.

jealously guarding the mysteries of their profession, but inviting the uninitiated, the public at large, to join them, having as one of its objects to break down those imaginary and hurtful barriers which exist between men of science and so-called men of practice—I felt that I could, from the peculiar position in which Providence has placed me in this country, appear as the representative of that large public, which profits by and admires your exertions, but is unable actively to join in them ; that my election was an act of humility on your part, which to reject would have looked like false humility—that is, like pride, on mine. But I reflected further, and saw in my acceptance the means, of which necessarily so few are offered to Her Majesty, of testifying to you, through the instrumentality of her husband, that your labours are not unappreciated by your Sovereign, and that she wishes her people to know this as well as yourselves. Guided by these reflections, my choice was speedily made, for the path of duty lay straight before me.

THE CRADLE OF POLITICAL ARITHMETIC.

I<small>T</small> is here that the idea of an International Statistical Congress took its origin, when delegates and visitors from all nations had assembled to exhibit in noble rivalry the products of their science, skill, and industry in the Great Exhibition of 1851 ; it is here that statistical science was earliest developed. Dr. Farr has well reminded us that England has been called, by no less an authority than Bernouilli, "the cradle of political arithmetic," and that we may even appeal to our Domesday Book as one of the most ancient and complete monuments of the science in existence. It is this country also which will and must derive the greatest benefits from the achievements of this science.

Old as your science is, and undeniable as are the benefits which it has rendered to mankind, it is yet little understood by the multitude ; it is new in its acknowledged position among the other

sciences, and still subject to many vulgar preju-
dices. It is little understood, for it is dry and
unpalatable to the general public in its simple
arithmetical expressions, representing living facts
(which as such are capable of arousing the liveliest
sympathy) in dry figures and tables for comparison.
Much labour is required to wade through endless
columns of figures, much patience to master them,
and some skill to draw any definite and safe
conclusions from the mass of material which they
present to the student; while the value of the information offered depends exactly upon its bulk,
increasing in proportion with its quantity and
comprehensiveness. It has been little understood,
also, from the peculiar and often unjustifiable
use which has been made of it; for the very fact
of its difficulty, and the patience required in
reading up and verifying the statistical figures
which may be referred to by an author in support of his theories and opinions, protect him,
to a certain extent, from scrutiny, and tempt him
to draw largely upon so convenient and available
a capital.

AIDS TO SCIENTIFIC OBSERVATION.

THE question how to observe resolvès itself into two—that of the scientific method which is to be employed in approaching a problem or in making an observation, and that of the philosophical instruments used in the observation or experiment. Our British Association brings to bear the combined knowledge and experience of the scientific men not only of this but of other countries on the discovery of that method, which, while it economises time and labour, promises the most accurate results. The method to which, after careful examination, the palm has been awarded, is then placed at the free disposal and use of all scientific investigators. It has also issued, where practicable, printed forms, merely requiring the different heads to be filled up, which, by their uniformity, become an important means for assisting the subsequent reduction of the observations for the abstraction of the laws which they may indicate. At the same time, most searching tests and inquiries are constantly carried on in the Observatory at Kew, given to the Association by Her Majesty, the object of which is practically to test the relative value of different methods and instruments, and to guide the constantly progressive improvements in the construction of the latter. The establishment at Kew has undertaken the further important service of verifying and correcting to a fixed standard the instruments of any maker, to enable observations made with them to be reduced to the same numerical expression.

THE EXHIBITION OF 1851.

THE Exhibition of 1851 is to give us a true test and a living picture of the point of development at which the whole of mankind has arrived in this grand task, and a new starting point from which all nations will be able to direct their further exertions.

I confidently hope that the first impression
which the view of this vast collection will produce
upon the spectator will be that of deep thank-
fulness to the Almighty for the blessings which
He has bestowed upon us already here below;
and the second, the conviction that they can only
be realized in proportion to the help which we
are prepared to render each other; therefore, only
by peace, love, and ready assistance, not only
between individuals, but between the nations of
the earth.

This being my conviction, I must be highly
gratified to see assembled the magistrates of all
the important towns of this realm, sinking all
their local and possible political differences, the
representatives of the different political opinions
of the country, and the representatives of the
different English nations, to-day representing only
one interest!

On *your* courage, perseverance, and liberality,
the undertaking now entirely depends.*   I feel
the strongest confidence in these qualities of the

* Spoken October 25, 1850.

British people, and I am sure that they will repose confidence in themselves—confidence that they will honourably sustain the contest of emulation, and that they will nobly carry out their proffered hospitality to their foreign competitors.

PUBLIC ENCOURAGEMENT OF SCIENCE.

THE impediments to the general progress of Science are of various kinds. If they were only such as direction, advice, and encouragement, would enable the individual, or even combined efforts of philosophers, to overcome, the exertions of the British Association might be sufficient for the purpose. But they are often such as can only be successfully dealt with by the powerful arm of the state or the long purse of the nation. These impediments may be caused either by the social condition of the country itself, by restrictions arising out of peculiar laws, by the political separation of different countries, or by the magnitude of the undertakings being out of all proportion to the means and power of single individuals, of the Association, or even the voluntary efforts of the public. In these cases the Association, together with its sister society, "the Royal Society," becomes the spokesman of Science with the Crown, the Government, or Parliament—sometimes even, through the Home Government, with foreign Governments. Thus it obtained the establishment, by the British Government, of magnetic and meteorological observatories in six different parts of the globe, as the beginning of a network of stations which we must hope will be so far extended as to compass by their geographical distribution the whole of the phenomena which throw light on this important point in our tellurian and even cosmical existence. The Institute of France, at the recommendation of M. Arago, whose loss the scientific world must long deplore, cheerfully co-operated with our Council on this occasion. It was our Association which, in conjunction with the Royal Society, suggested the Antarctic Expedition, with a view to further the discovery of the laws of terrestrial magnetism, and thus led to the discovery of the southern polar continent. It urged on the Admiralty the prosecution of the tidal observations, which that department has since fully carried out. It recommended the establishment, in the British Museum, of the Conchological Collection, exhibiting present and extinct species, which has now become an object of the greatest interest.

———————

THE EDINBURGH NATIONAL GALLERY.

THE building, of which we have just begun the foundation,* is a temple to be erected to the Fine Arts, which have so important an influence upon the development of the mind and feeling of a people, and which are so generally taken as the type of the degree and character of that development, that it is on the fragments of works of art, come down to us from bygone nations, that we

* The Edinburgh National Gallery.

are wont to form our estimate of the state of
their civilization, manners, customs, and religion.

Let us hope that the impulse given to the
culture of the Fine Arts in this country, and the
daily increasing attention bestowed upon it by the
people at large, will not only tend to refine and
elevate the national tastes, but will also lead to
the production of works, which, if left behind us
as memorials of our age, will give to after generations an adequate idea of our advanced state of
civilization.

It must be an additional source of gratification
to me to find that part of the funds rendered
available for the support of this undertaking
should be the ancient grant which, at the union
of the two kingdoms, was secured towards the
encouragement of the fisheries and manufactures
of Scotland, as it affords a most pleasing proof
that those important branches of industry have
arrived at that state of manhood and prosperity,
when, no longer requiring the aid of a fostering
government, they can maintain themselves inde-
pendently, relying upon their own vigour and

activity, and can now in their turn lend assistance and support to their younger and weaker sisters, the Fine Arts.

The history of this grant exhibits to us the picture of a most healthy national progress; the ruder arts connected with the necessaries of life, *first* gaining strength; then education and science supervening and directing further exertions : and lastly, the arts which only adorn life becoming longed for by a prosperous and educated people.

May nothing disturb this progress, and may, by God's blessing, that peace and prosperity be preserved to the nation which will insure to it a long continuance of moral and intellectual enjoyment.

THE CITY OF ABERDEEN AND THE STUDY OF PHILOSOPHY.

THE Poet, in his works of fiction, has to choose, and anxiously to weigh, where to lay his scene, knowing that, like the Painter, he is thus laying in the background of his picture, which will give tone and colour to the whole.   The stern and dry reality of life is governed by the same laws, and we are here* living, feeling, and thinking, under the influence of the local impressions of this northern seaport.   The choice appears to be a good one.   The travelling philosophers have to come far, but in approaching the Highlands of Scotland they meet nature in its wild and primitive form, and nature is the object of their studies.   The geologist will not find many novelties in yonder mountains, because he will stand there on the bare backbone of the globe; but the primary rocks, which stand out in their nakedness, exhibit the grandeur and beauty of their peculiar form, and in the splendid quarries of this neighbourhood are seen to peculiar advantage the closeness and hardness of their mass, and their inexhaustible supply for the use of man, made vaailable by the application of new mechanical powers.   On this primitive soil the botanist and zoologist will be attracted only by a limited range

* Spoken at the meeting of the British Association, held in Aberdeen in 1859.

of plants and animals, but they are the very species which the extension of agriculture and increase of population are gradually driving out of many parts of the country. On those blue hills the red deer, in vast herds, holds undisturbed dominion over the wide heathery forest, until the sportsman, fatigued and unstrung by the busy life of the bustling town, invades the moor, to regain health and vigour by measuring his strength with that of the antlered monarch of the hill. But, notwithstanding all his efforts to overcome an antagonist possessed of such superiority of power, swiftness, caution, and keenness of all the senses, the sportsman would find himself baffled, had not Science supplied him with the telescope and those terrible weapons which seem daily to progress in the precision with which they carry the deadly bullet, mocking distance, to the mark.

In return for the help which Science has afforded him, the sportsman can supply the naturalist with many facts which he alone has opportunity of observing, and which may assist the solution of some interesting problems sug-

F

gested by the life of the deer. Man, also, the highest object of our study, is found in vigorous, healthy development, presenting a happy mixture of the Celt, Goth, Saxon, and Dane, acquiring his strength on the hills and the sea. The Aberdeen whaler braves the icy regions of the Polar Sea, to seek and to battle with the great monster of the deep : he has materially assisted in opening these icebound regions to the researches of Science; he fearlessly aided in the search after Sir John Franklin and his gallant companions, whom their country sent forth on this mission ; but to whom Providence, alas! has denied the reward of their labours, the return to their homes, to the affectionate embrace of their families and friends, and the acknowledgments of a grateful nation. The city of Aberdeen itself is rich in interest for the philosopher. Its two lately united Universities make it a seat of learning and science. The collection of antiquities, formed for the present occasion, enables him to dive into olden times, and, by contact with the remains of the handiworks of the ancient inhabitants of Scotland, to

enter into the spirit of that peculiar and interesting people, which has always attracted the attention and touched the hearts of men accessible to
the influence of heroic poetry. The Spalding
Club, founded in this city, for the preservation of
the historical and literary remains of the north-
eastern counties of Scotland, is honourably known
by its important publications.

––––––––

*IMPORTANCE TO SCIENCE OF INTERNATIONAL
COMMUNICATION.*

THE importance of these international statistical
congresses cannot be overrated. They not only
awaken public attention to the value of these
pursuits, bring together men of all countries who
devote their lives to them, and who are thus
enabled to exchange their thoughts and varied
experiences ; but they pave the way to an agreement among many different governments and
nations, to follow up these common inquiries, in

a common spirit, by a common method, and for a common end. It is only in the largest number of observations that the law becomes apparent, and the truth becomes more and more to be relied upon, the larger the amount of facts ˙accurately observed which form the basis of its elucidation. It is consequently of the highest importance that observations identical in character should embrace the largest field of observation attainable. It is not sufficient, however, to collect the statistical facts of one class over the greatest area and to the fullest amount ; but we require, in order to arrive at sound conclusions as to the influences producing these facts, the statistics of the increase of population, of marriages, births, and deaths, of emigration, disease, crime, education, and occupatiou, of the products of agriculture, mining, and manufacture, of the results of trade, commerce, and finance. Nor, while their comparison becomes an essential element in the investigation of our socia condition, does it suffice to obtain these observations as a whole, but we require also, and particularly, the comparison of these same classes of facts in different countries, under the varying influences of political and religious conditions, of occupation, races, and climates.

―――――

POWER OF PUBLIC OPINION.

PUBLIC opinion is the powerful lever which in these days moves a people for good and for evil, and to public opinion we must therefore appeal if we would achieve any lasting and beneficial results.

―――――

INFLUENCES OF CRITICISM ON ART.

THE production of all works in art or poetry requires in their conception and execution not only an exercise of the intellect, skill, and patience, but particularly a concurrent warmth of feeling and a free flow of imagination. This renders them most tender plants, which will thrive only in an atmosphere calculated to maintain that warmth, and that atmosphere is one of kindness—kindness towards the artist personally as well as towards his production. An unkind word of criticism passes like a cold blast over their tender shoots, and shrivels them up, checking the flow of the sap, which was rising to produce, perhaps, multitudes of flowers and fruit. But still, criticism is absolutely necessary to the development of art, and the injudicious praise of an inferior work becomes an insult to superior genius.

EVIL EFFECTS OF TRADE IN ART.

OUR times are peculiarly unfavourable when compared with those when Madonnas were painted in the seclusion of convents ; for we have now, on the one hand, the eager competition of a vast array of artists of every degree of talent and skill, and on the other, as judge, a great public, for the greater part wholly uneducated in art, and thus led by professional writers, who often strive to impress the public with a great idea of their own artistic knowledge by the merciless manner in which they treat works which cost those who produced them the highest efforts of mind or feeling.

The works of art, by being publicly exhibited and offered for sale, are becoming articles of trade, following as such the unreasoning laws of markets and fashion ; and public and even private patronage is swayed by their tyrannical influence.

ALEXANDER VON HUMBOLDT.

ALEXANDER VON HUMBOLDT incessantly strove after dominion over that universality of human knowledge which stands in need of thoughtful government and direction to preserve its integrity ; he strove to tie up the fasces of scientific knowledge to give them strength in unity. He treated all scientific men as members of one family, enthusiastically directing, fostering, and encouraging inquiry, where he saw either the want of or the willingness for it.   His protection of the young and ardent student led many to success in their pursuit.   His personal influence with the courts and governments of most countries in Europe enabled him to plead the cause of Science in a manner which made it more difficult for them to refuse than to grant what he requested.   All lovers of science deeply mourn for the loss of such a man.

THE OLD PARISH SCHOOL.*

LOOKING to former times, we find that our forefathers, with their wonted piety and paternal care, had established a system of national education, based upon the parish organization and forming part of parish life, which met the wants

* This and the next five paragraphs, which must be read in connexion with each other, are extracted from an address delivered on the 22d June, 1857, at the Conference on National Education.

of their day, and had in it a certain unity and completeness which we might well envy at the present moment. But in the progress of time our wants have outstripped that system, and the condition of the country has so completely changed even within these last fifty years, that the old parochial division is no longer adequate for the present population. This has increased during that period in England and Wales from, in round numbers, 9,000,000 to 18,000,000, and, where there formerly existed comparatively small towns and villages, we now see mighty cities like Liverpool, Manchester, Hull, Leeds, Birmingham, and others, with their hundreds of thousands, springing up almost as it were by enchantment; London having increased nearly two and a half millions of souls, and the factory district of Lancashire alone having aggregated a population of nearly three millions within a radius of thirty miles.

THE ENGLISHMAN'S JEALOUSY OF CONTROL.

THIS change could not escape the watchful eye of a patriotic public; but how to provide the means of satisfying the new wants could not be a matter of easy solution. While zeal for the public good, a fervent religious spirit, and true philanthropy, are qualities eminently distinguishing our countrymen, the love of liberty, and an aversion from being controlled by the power of the State in matters nearest to their hearts, are feelings which will always most powerfully influence them in action. Thus, the common object has been contemplated from the most different points of view, and pursued often upon antagonistic principles. Some have sought the aid of Government, others that of the Church to which they belong; some have declared it to be the duty of the State to provide elementary instruction for the people at large; others have seen in State interference a check to the spontaneous exertions of the people themselves, and an interference with self-government; some again have advocated a plan of compulsory education based upon local self-government, and others the voluntary system in its widest development. While these have been some of the political subjects of difference, those in the religious field have not been less marked and potent. We find on the one hand the wish to see secular and religious instruction separated, and the former recognised as an innate and inherent right, to which each member of society has a claim, and which ought not to be denied to him if he refuses to take along with it the inculcation of a particular dogma to which he objects as unsound; while we see, on the other hand, the doctrine asserted that no education can be sound which does not rest on religious instruction, and that religious truth is too sacred to be modified and tampered with, even in its minutest deductions, for the sake of procuring a general agreement.

ADVANTAGES OF A NEUTRAL GROUND.

I_F these differences were to have been discussed here to-day, I should not have been
able to respond to your invitation to take the
chair, as I should have thought it inconsistent
with the position which I occupy, and with the
duty which I owe to the Queen and country at
large. I see those here before me who have
taken a leading part in these important discussions, and I am happy to meet them upon a
neutral ground; happy to find that there is a
neutral ground upon which their varied talents
and abilities can be brought to bear in com-
munion upon the common object; and proud
and grateful to them that they should have
allowed me to preside over them for the purpose
of working together in the common vineyard. I
feel certain that the greatest benefit must arise to
the cause we have all so much at heart, by the
mere free exchange of your thoughts and various
experience.

STARTLING FACTS.

You may well be proud, gentlemen, of the results hitherto achieved by your rival efforts, and may point to the fact that, since the beginning of the century, while the population has doubled itself, the number of schools both public and private has been multiplied 14 times. In 1801, there were in England and Wales of public schools 2,876; of private schools, 487—total, 3,363. In 1851 (the year of the census), there were in England and Wales—of public schools, 15,518; of private schools, 30,524—total, 46,042; giving instruction in all to 2,144,378 scholars; of whom 1,422,982 belong to public schools, and 721,396 to the private schools. The rate of progress is further illustrated by statistics, which show that in 1818 the proportion of day scholars to the population was 1 in 17; in 1833, 1 in 11; and in 1851, 1 in 8. These are great results, although I hope they may only be received as

instalments of what has yet to be done.   But
what must be your feelings when you reflect upon
the fact, the inquiry into which has brought us
together, that this great boon thus obtained for
the mass of the people, and which is freely offered
to them, should have been only partially accepted,
and, upon the whole, so insufficiently applied, as
to render its use almost valueless.   We are told,
that the total population in England and Wales
of children between the ages of 3 and 15 being
estimated at 4,908,696, only 2,046,848 attend school
at all, while 2,861,848 receive no instruction what-
ever.   At the same time, an analysis of the scholars
with reference to the length of time allowed for
their school tuition shows that 42 per cent. of
them have been at school less than one year,
22 per cent. during one year, 15 per cent. during
two years, 9 per cent. during three years, 5 per
cent. during four years, and 4 per cent. during
five years.   Therefore, out of the two millions of
scholars alluded to, more than one million and a
half remain only two years at school.   I leave it
to you to judge what the results of such an educa-

tion can be. I find, further, that of these two millions of children attending school, only about six hundred thousand are above the age of nine. These are startling facts, which render it evident that no extension of the means of education will be of any avail, unless this evil which lies at the root of the whole question be removed, and that it is high time that the country should become thoroughly awake to its existence, and prepared to meet it energetically.

THE-ROOT OF A GREAT EVIL.

YOU will richly add to the services you have already rendered to the noble cause if you will prepare public opinion by your inquiry into this state of things, and by discussing in your sections the causes of it as well as their remedies which may lie within our reach. This will be no easy matter ; but even if your labours should not result in the adoption of any immediate practical steps, you will have done great good in preparing for them. It will probably happen that, in this instance as in most others, the cause which produces the evil will be more easily detected than its remedy, and yet a just appreciation of the former must ever be the first and essential condition for the discovery of the latter. You will probably trace the cause of our social condition to a state of ignorance and lethargic indifference on the subject among parents generally; but the root of the evil will, I suspect, be found to extend into that field on which the political economist exercises his activity—I mean the labour market—demand and supply. To dissipate that ignorance and rouse from that lethargy may be difficult, but with the united and earnest efforts of all who are the friends of the working classes it ought, after all, to be only a question of time.

THE POOR MAN'S CHILDREN.

WHAT measures can be brought to bear upon the other root of the evil is a more delicate question, and will require the nicest care in handling, for there you cut into the very quick of the working man's condition. His children are not only his offspring, to be reared for a future independent position, but they constitute part of his productive power, and work with him for the staff of life; the daughters especially are the handmaids of the house, the assistants of the mother, the nurses of the younger children, the aged, and the sick. To deprive the labouring family of their help would be almost to paralyse its domestic existence. On the other hand, carefully collected statistics reveal to us the fact that while about 600,000 children between the ages of three and fifteen are absent from school, but known to be employed, no less than 2,200,000 are not at schools, whose absence cannot be traced to any

G

ascertained employment or other legitimate cause. You will have to work, then, upon the minds and hearts of the parents, to place before them the irreparable mischief which they inflict upon those who are entrusted to their care by keeping them from the light of knowledge, to bring home to their conviction that it is their duty to exert themselves for their children's education, bearing in mind at the same time that it is not only their most sacred duty, but also their highest privilege. Unless they work with you, your work, our work, will be vain ; but you will not fail, I feel sure, in obtaining their co-operation if you remind them of their duty to their God and Creator.

SERVANTS' SAVINGS.

ALTHOUGH this wise and benevolent measure * has been enacted so long ago as the third year of the reign of King William IV., I find, to my deep regret, that during the whole time, only

* The "Deferred Annuities Act."

about 600 persons have availed themselves of its provisions. I can discover no other reason for this inadequate success, but that the existence of the Act is not generally known, or that people are afraid of Law and Acts of Parliament, which they cannot understand on account of their complicated technical wording. I have heard another reason stated, to which, however, I give little credit, namely, that servants fear lest a knowledge that they are able to purchase annuities by savings from their wages, might induce their masters to reduce them. I have a better opinion of the disposition of employers generally, and am convinced that on the contrary nothing counteracts more the liberality of masters than the idea, not wholly unfounded, that an increase of means, instead of prompting to saving, leads to extravagance.

NEGLECT OF SCIENTIFIC STUDIES.

Is it to be wondered at, that the interests of science, abstract as science appears, and not immediately showing a return in pounds, shillings, and pence, should be postponed, at least, to others which promise immediate tangible results? Is it to be wondered at, that even our public men require an effort to wean themselves from other subjects in order to give their attention to science and men of science, when it is remembered that science, with the exception of mathematics, was until of late almost systematically excluded from our school and university education; that the traditions of early life are those which make and leave the strongest impression on the human mind, and that the subjects with which we become acquainted, and to which our energies are devoted in youth, are those for which we retain the liveliest interest in after years, and that for these reasons the effort required must be both a mental and a moral one?

THE CHURCH OF ENGLAND.

WHILST we have to congratulate ourselves upon our state of temporal prosperity, harmony at home, and peace abroad, we cannot help deploring that the Church, whose exertions for the progress of Christianity and civilization we are to-day acknowledging, should be afflicted by internal dissensions and attacks from without. I have no fear, however, for her safety and ultimate welfare so long as she holds fast to what our ancestors gained for us at the Reformation, the Gospel and the unfettered right of its use.

The dissensions and difficulties which we witness in this as in every other Church, arise from the natural and necessary conflict of the two antagonistic principles which move human society in Church as well as in State; I mean the principles of individual liberty and of allegiance and submission to the will of the community, exacted by it for its own preservation.

These conflicting principles cannot safely be disregarded : they must be reconciled. To this country belongs the honour of having succeeded in this mighty task, as far as the State is concerned, whilst other nations are still wrestling with it ; and I feel persuaded that the same earnest zeal and practical wisdom which have made her political constitution an object of admiration to other nations will, under God's blessing, make her Church likewise a model to the world.

Let us look upon this assembly as a token of future hope, and may the harmony which reigns amongst us at this moment, and which we owe to having met in furtherance of a common holy object, be by the Almighty permanently bestowed upon the Church.

AGRICULTURAL STATISTICS.

· WE hope to lay before you,* as far as Great
Britain is concerned, the Registrar-General's analysis of the causes of death, and the dangers
that people encounter at each period of life;
complete returns of the produce of our mines;
the agricultural returns of Ireland, in which the
Registrar-General of that country has given every
year the breadth of land under every kind of
crop, with an estimate of its produce, and has
proved by his success in obtaining these facts
at a comparatively moderate expense, and by the
voluntary assistance of the landowners and cultivators, as well as of the clergy of all denomina-
tions, that the apprehension was groundless, that
it could not be done without cost, or without
injuring individual interests. We must hope that,
considering its importance with regard to all ques-

* This and the next paragraphs are from the address
delivered before the International Statistical Congress,
July 16, 1860.

tions affecting the food of the people, this inquiry will not only be extended to England and Scotland, but also to the Continent generally, wherever it may not already have been instituted. Our trade returns will exhibit the great effects produced on our commerce by the changes in our commercial system ; our colonial delegates will exhibit to you proofs of the wonderful progress of their countries, and proofs at the same time that elaborate statistics have rendered them conscious of that progress. And I have no doubt that the foreign delegates will more than repay us by the information which they will give us in exchange.

OUR DEPENDENCE ON EACH OTHER.

THESE returns will, no doubt, prove to us afresh in figures what we know already from feeling and from experience, how dependent the different nations are upon each other for their progress, for their moral and material prosperity, and that the essential condition of their mutual happiness is the maintenance of peace and good-will among each other. Let them still be rivals in the noble race of social improvement, in which, although it may be the lot of one to arrive first at the goal, yet all will equally share the prize, all feeling their own powers and strength increase in the healthy competition.

IMPORTANCE OF UNIFORMITY.

I TRUST that it will not be thought pre-sumptuous in me if I exhort you generally not to lose yourselves in points of minute detail, how-ever tempting and attractive they may be from their intrinsic interest and importance; but to direct your undivided energies to the establish-ment of those broad principles upon which the common action of different nations can be based, which common action must be effected if we are to make real progress. I know that this Congress can only suggest and recommend, and that it must ultimately rest with the different Governments to carry out those suggestions. Many previous recommendations, it is true, have been carried out, but many have been left unattended to, and I will not except our own country from blame in this respect.

A PRAYER FOR THE SPREAD OF TRUTH.

HAPPY and proud indeed should I feel if this noble gathering should be enabled to lay the solid foundation of an edifice, necessarily slow of construction, and requiring for generations to come laborious and persevering exertion, intended as it is for the promotion of human happiness by leading to the discovery of those eternal laws upon which that universal happiness is dependent. May He who has implanted in our hearts a craving after the discovery of truth, and given us our reasoning faculties to the end that we should use them for this discovery, sanctify our efforts and bless them in their results.

AN AGRICULTURAL SHOW.

SOME years have elapsed already since I last dined with you in this migratory pavilion, and I am glad that you should have pitched it this day under the walls of Windsor Castle, and that I should myself have an opportunity of bidding you a hearty welcome in the Home Park.*

Your encampment singularly contrasts with that which the barons of England, the feudal lords of the land, with their retainers, erected round old Windsor Castle on a similar mead, though not exactly in the same locality. They came then clad in steel, with lance and war-horse; you appear in a more peaceful attire, and the animals you bring with you are the tokens of your successful cultivation of the arts of peace. King John came trembling amongst his subjects, unwillingly compelled to sign that great charter

* From the speech at the Royal Agricultural Society's Show, July 16, 1851.

which has ever since been your birthright. Your sovereign came confiding among her loyal and loving people; she came to admire the results of their industry, and to encourage them to persevere in their exertions.

And the gratification which the Queen has felt at the sight of your splendid collection must, I am sure, be participated in by all who examine it.

————————

THE CLERGY AS HUSBANDS AND FATHERS.

When our ancestors purified the Christian faith, and shook off the yoke of a domineering priesthood, they felt that the key-stone of that wonderful fabric which had grown up in the dark times of the middle ages was the celibacy of the clergy, and shrewdly foresaw that their reformed faith and newly-won religious liberty would, on the contrary, only be secure in the hands of a clergy united with the people by every sympathy, national, personal, and domestic.

This nation has enjoyed for three hundred years the blessings of a Church establishment, which rests upon this basis, and cannot be too grateful for the advantages afforded by the fact that the Christian ministers not only preach the doctrines of Christianity, but live among their congregations an example for the discharge of every Christian duty, as husbands, fathers, and masters of families, themselves capable of fathoming the whole depth of human feelings, desires, and difficulties.

Whilst we must gratefully acknowledge that they have, as a body, worthily fulfilled this high and difficult task, we must bear in mind that we deny them an equal participation in one of the actuating motives of life—the one which, amongst the "children of this generation," exercises, perhaps of necessity, the strongest influence—I mean the desire for the acquisition and accumulation of the goods of this world.

The appellation of a "money-making parson" is not only a reproach, but a condemnation for a clergyman, depriving him at once of all influence over his congregation. Yet this man, who has to shun opportunities for acquiring wealth open to most of us, and who has himself only an often scanty life-income allotted to him for his services, has a wife and children like ourselves ; and we wish him to have the same solicitude for their welfare which we feel for our own.

MERITORIOUS "BORES."

I WILL merely express my satisfaction that there should exist bodies of men who will bring the well-considered and understood wants of science before the public and the Government; who will even hand round the begging-box, and expose themselves to refusals and rebuffs to which all beggars are liable, with the certainty besides of being considered great bores. Please to recollect that this species of bore is a most useful animal, well adapted for the ends for which Nature intended him. He alone, by constantly returning to the charge, and repeating the same truths and the same requests, succeeds in awakening attention to the cause which he advocates, and obtains that hearing which is granted him at last for self-protection, as the minor evil compared to his importunity, but which is requisite to make his cause understood. This is more particularly the case in a free, active, enterprising, and self-determining people like ours, where every interest works for itself, considers itself the all-important one, and makes its way in the world by its own efforts.

GROWTH OF LONDON.

A CERTAIN dislocation of habits and interests must inevitably attend the removal of the great City market* from the site it has occupied for so many centuries, and this may possibly retard for the moment the fullest development of the undertaking; but any opposition arising from such

* From the address on the opening of the Metropolitan Cattle Market.

causes will soon cease, and the farmers will, doubt-
less, soon learn to appreciate the boon thus conferred upon them by the Corporation of London,
in the increased facility which will be afforded to
them for the transaction of their business, and the
comparative security with which they will be
enabled to bring up and display their valuable
stock in the Great Metropolitan Cattle Market.

This wonderful metropolis, which has already
gathered beneath its roofs nearly two millions and
a half of human beings, and has even within these
last six years added not less than 290 miles of
street to its extent, imperatively requires that those
establishments which are to minister to the common wants of the whole should keep pace with
its growth and magnitude. They can only be
undertaken by public bodies, they can only be
successfully carried out by public spirit. I know
that the difficulties which have to be overcome,
where so much private capital has acquired vested
interests, are immense ; but I hail the spirit which
is rising amongst us, and which, I doubt not, will
meet those difficulties.

THE OLD ENGLISH HABIT.

THE Statistical Congress of All Nations * has been invited by the Government to hold its fourth meeting in this metropolis, in conformity with the wishes expressed by the late Congress held at Vienna, in 1857. Although, under these circumstances, it would have been more properly within the province of a member of the Government and minister of the Crown to fill this chair and open the proceedings of the day, as has been the case in previous meetings of the Congress in other places, the nature of the institutions and the habits of the people of the country in which this assembly was to take place, could not fail to make itself felt, and to influence its organization. We are a people possessing and enjoying the most intense political life, in which every question of interest or importance to the nation is publicly canvassed and debated. The whole nation, as it were, from the

* Held in London, in July, 1860.

H

highest to the lowest, takes an active part in these debates, and arrives at a judgment on the collective result of the thoughts and opinions thus called forth. This Congress could, therefore, only be either a private meeting of the delegates of different Governments, discussing special questions of interest in the midst of the general bustle of political activity, or it had to assume a public and a national character, addressing itself to the public at large, and inviting its co-operation.

The Government have chosen the latter alternative, and have been met by the readiest response from all sides. They have, I think, wisely chosen ; for it is of the utmost importance to the object the Congress has in view, namely, not only the diffusion of statistical information, but also the acquisition of a general acknowledgment of the usefulness and importance of this branch of human knowledge—that the public, as a whole, should lend its powerful aid.

SCIENCE, ART, AND INDUSTRY.

IT has been a great pleasure to me to have been able to participate, in however trifling a degree, in a work which I do not look upon as a simple act of worldly wisdom on the part of this great town and locality, but as one of the first public acknowledgments of a principle which is daily forcing its way amongst us, and is destined to play a great and important part in the future development of this nation and of the world in general; I mean the introduction of science and art, as the conscious regulators of productive industry.

SELF-RELIANCE AND THE WORKING CLASSES.

I CONCEIVE that this Society* is founded upon a right principle, as it follows out the dictates of a correct appreciation of human nature, which requires every man, by personal exertion, and

* The Servants' Provident Society.

according to his own choice, to work out his own happiness; which prevents his valuing, nay, even his feeling satisfaction at, the prosperity which others have made for him.   It is founded upon a right principle, because it endeavours to trace out a plan according to which, by providence, by present self-denial and perseverance, not only will the servant be raised in his physical and moral condition, but the master also will be taught how to direct his efforts in aiding the servant in his labour to secure to himself resources in cases of sickness, old age, and want of employment.   It is founded on a right principle, because in its financial scheme there is no temptation held out to the servant, by the prospect of possible extra-vagant advantages, which tend to transform his providence into a species of gambling; by con-vivial meetings which lead him to ulterior expense; or by the privilege of balloting for the few prizes, which draws him into all the waste of time and excitement of an electioneering contest.

Such are the characteristics of several insti-tutions, upon which servants and many of our other industrial classes place their reliance. And what can be more heartrending than to witness the breaking of banks, and the failure of such institutions, which not only mar the prospects of these unhappy people, and plunge them into sudden destitution, but destroy in others all confidence in the honesty or sagacity of those who preach to them the advantages of providence.

Let them well consider that if they must embark in financial speculations, if they like to have convivial meetings, if they claim the right of governing the concerns of their own body, they must not risk for this, in one stake, their whole future existence, the whole prosperity of their families. Let them always bear in mind, that their savings are capital, that capital will only return a certain interest, and that any advantage offered beyond that interest has to be purchased at a commensurate risk of the capital itself.

THE PRINCIPLES OF BEAUTY.

THE fine arts (as far as they relate to painting, sculpture, and architecture), which are sometimes confounded with art in general, rest on the application of the laws of form and colour, and what may be called the science of the beautiful. They do not rest on any arbitrary theory on the modes of producing pleasurable emotions, but follow fixed laws—more difficult perhaps to seize than those regulating the material world, because belonging partly to the sphere of the ideal, and of our spiritual essence, yet perfectly appreciable and teachable, both abstractedly and historically, from the works of different ages and nations.

VALUE OF SCIENTIFIC CONGRESSES.

THIS is not the thoughtful direction of one mind over acquired knowledge, but the production of new thought by the contact of many minds, as the spark is produced by the friction of flint and steel; it is not the action of the monarchy of a paternal government, but the republican activity of the Roman Forum. These meetings draw forth the philosopher from the hidden recesses of his study, call in the wanderer over the field of science to meet his brethren, to lay before them the results of his labours, to set forth the deductions at which he has arrived, to ask for their examination, to maintain in the combat of debate the truth of his positions and the accuracy of his observations. These meetings, unlike those of any other society, throw open the arena to the cultivators of all sciences, to their mutual advantage: the geologist learns from the chemist that there are problems for which he had no clue, but which that science can solve for him; the geographer receives light from the naturalist, the astronomer from the physicist and engineer, and so on. And all find a field upon which to meet the public at large, invite them to listen to their reports, and even to take part in their discussions—show to them that philosophers are not vain theorists, but essentially men of practice—not conceited pedants, wrapped up in their own mysterious importance, but humble inquirers after truth, proud only of what they may have achieved or won for the general use of man. Neither are they daring and presumptuous unbelievers—a character which ignorance has sometimes affixed to them—who would, like the Titans, storm heaven by placing mountain upon mountain, till hurled down from the height attained by the terrible thunders of outraged Jove; but rather the pious pilgrims to the Holy Land, who toil on in search of the sacred shrine, in search of truth—God's truth—God's laws as manifested in His works, in His creation.

THE LAWS OF NATURE.

THE courage and spirit of enterprise with which an immense amount of capital is embarked in industrial pursuits, and the skill and indefatigable perseverance with which these are carried on in this country, cannot but excite universal admiration ; but in all our operations, whether agricultural or manufacturing, it is not *we* who operate, but the laws of nature, which we have set in operation.

It is, then, of the highest importance that we should know these laws, in order to know what we are about, and the reason why certain things are, which occur daily under our hands, and what course we are to pursue with regard to them.

Without such knowledge, we are condemned to one of three states : either we merely go on to do things just as our fathers did, and for no better reason than because they did them so ; or, trusting to some personal authority, we adopt at random the recommendation of some specific, in a speculative hope that it may answer; or, lastly—and this is the most favourable case—we ourselves improve upon certain processes; but this can only be the result of an experience hardly earned and dearly bought, and which, after all, can only embrace a comparatively short space of time, and a small number of experiments.

From none of these causes can we hope for much progress; for the mind, however ingenious, has no materials to work with, and remains so in presence of phenomena, the causes of which are hidden from it.

But these laws of nature, these Divine laws, are capable of being discovered and understood, and of being taught and made our own. This is the task of science; and, whilst science discovers and teaches these laws, art teaches their application. No pursuit is therefore too insignificant not to be capable of becoming the subject both of a science and an art.

GENIUS MADE FRUITFUL BY KNOWLEDGE.

FAR be it from me to undervalue the creative power of genius, or to treat shrewd common sense as worthless without knowledge. But nobody will tell me that the same genius would not take an incomparably higher flight, if supplied with all the means which knowledge can impart, or that common sense does not become, in fact, only truly powerful, when in possession of the materials upon which judgment is to be exercised.

IMPORTANCE OF THE STUDY OF THE ARTS AND SCIENCES.

THE study of the laws by which the Almighty governs the universe is our bounden duty. Of these laws our great academies and seats of education have, rather arbitrarily, selected only two spheres or groups, as I may call them, as essential parts of our national education : the laws which regulate quantities and proportions, which form the subject of mathematics ; and the laws regulating the expression of our thoughts, through the medium of language, that is to say, grammar, which finds its purest expression in the classical languages.   These laws are most important branches of knowledge, their study tráins and elevates the mind, but they are not the only ones ; there are others which we cannot disregard, which we cannot do without.

There are, for instance, the laws governing the human mind, and its relation to the Divine Spirit (the subject of logic and metaphysics); there are those which govern our bodily nature and its connexion with the soul (the subject of physiology and psychology) ; those which govern human society, and the relations between man and man (the subjects of politics, jurisprudence, and political economy), and many others.

Whilst of the laws just mentioned some have been recognised as essentials of education in different institutions, and some will, by the course of time, more fully assert their right to recognition, the laws regulating matter and form are those which will constitute the chief object of your pursuits; and, as the principle of subdivision of labour is the one most congenial to our age, I would advise you* to keep to this speciality, and to follow with undivided attention chiefly the sciences of mechanics, physics, and chemistry, and the fine arts in painting, sculpture, and architecture.

You will thus have conferred an inestimable boon upon your country, and in a short time have the satisfaction of witnessing the beneficial results upon our national powers of production. Other parts of the country will, I doubt not, emulate your example; and I live in hope that all these institutions will some day find a central point of union, and thus complete their national organization.

* Addressed to the members of the Birmingham Institute.

A GOOD WORK.

I REJOICE at the opportunity* which has this day been afforded to me of visiting this noble establishment, and my satisfaction in doing so is increased by the circumstance that my visit occurs at a period of its existence when the state of useful development to which by your exertions it has attained is about, by a continuance of the same exertions, to receive a still wider extension. In the progress of these schools, struggling, I may say, from the most lowly and humble beginnings up to their present and noble dimensions, we find a striking exemplification of the Divine truth, that the principle of good once sown is not destined to remain dormant, but that, like the grain of mustard-seed, it is calculated to extend and develop itself in an ever-increasing sphere of usefulness; and we may confidently hope that what you have now effected, following this uni-

* The opening of St. Thomas' Charterhouse Schools.

versal law, will not be limited in its results to the immediate objects of your charitable exertions, but that it will prove the means of diffusing untold blessings among the most remote generations. For you, Mr. Rogers, who have been mainly instrumental, and at great personal sacrifice, in bringing about this great good, and for those who have stood by you, and contributed by their support to the success of your efforts, there can, I am sure, be no higher source of gratification than in the contemplation of your own work. The reflection that you have been the instrument, under Divine Providence, of conferring upon the poor and needy in this vast district that greatest of all boons, the means of obtaining for their children the blessings of education and of religious instruction, without which any lasting success in life or any permanent amelioration of their lot would seem hopeless ; and still farther, the feeling that this inestimable blessing will be secured in a yet higher degree to their children's children, will carry with it its own best reward. Still it will be a source of legitimate pride and satisfaction to you

to know that your labours have not been un-
observed, but that your noble and Christianlike
exertions to benefit those who cannot help themselves have attracted the notice and admiration of
your Sovereign, and of those who are deputed
under her to watch over and promote the education and moral welfare of her people. The means
which you have adopted to effect your work of
benevolence appear no less deserving of commen-
dation than the object itself. You have not been
content with the bare attempt to force, perhaps
upon unwilling recipients, a boon, the value of
which might not be appreciated, but you have
wisely sought to work upon the convictions of the
parents of the children you wish to benefit, by
extending your assistance only to those who, by a
small contribution out of their hardly-won earn-
ings, have proved that they are awake to a sense
of the vast importance it is to their offspring that
the means of being fitted to pass successfully
through life, and by honest industry to better their
worldly condition, should be brought within their
reach. It is a source of high personal gratifica-

tion to me that I have been enabled, by my presence here this day, and by that of the Prince of
Wales, to mark, not only my own appreciation of
your labours, but also the deep interest which the
Queen takes in the well-being of the poorest of
her subjects ; and that gratification will be greatly
enhanced if by this public expression of the
sympathy of the Queen and of her family and
Government this noble cause shall be still further
advanced. Most earnestly do I pray that the
same success which has hitherto blessed your
labours may continue to attend your future progress, and that your example may stimulate other
localities to emulate your useful efforts.

THE NATURE OF SCIENCE.

To define the nature of Science, to give an
exact and complete definition of what Science
is and means, has, as it naturally must, at all
times occupied the Metaphysician. He has
answered the question in various ways, more or

less satisfactorily to himself or others. To me, Science, in its most general and comprehensive acceptation, means the knowledge of what I know, —the consciousness of human knowledge. Hence, to know is the object of all Science ; and all special knowledge, if brought to our consciousness in its separate distinctiveness from, and yet in its recognised relation to, the totality of our knowledge, is scientific knowledge. We require, then, for Science—that is to say, for the acquisition of scientific knowledge—those two activities of our mind which are necessary for the acquisition of *any* knowledge—analysis and synthesis : the first to dissect and reduce into its component parts the object to be investigated, and to render an accurate account to ourselves of the nature and qualities of these parts by observation ; the second to recompose the observed and understood parts into a unity in our consciousness, exactly answering to the object of our investigation.

TENDENCY TO CREATE NEW SCIENCES.

THE operation of Science has been, systematically to divide human knowledge, and raise, as it
were, the separate groups of subjects for scientific
consideration into different and distinct sciences.
The tendency to create new sciences is peculiarly
apparent in our present age, and it is perhaps inseparable from so rapid a progress as we have seen
in our days; for the acquaintance with and master-
ing of distinct branches of knowledge enables the
eye, from the newly gained points of sight, to see
the new ramifications into which they divide themselves in strict consecutiveness and with logical
necessity.   But in thus gaining new centres of
light, from which to direct our researches, and
new and powerful means of adding to its ever-
increasing treasures, Science approaches no nearer
to the limits of its range, although travelling
further and further from its original point of
departure.   For God's world is infinite; and the

boundlessness of the universe, whose confines appear ever to retreat before our finite minds, strikes us no less with awe when, prying into the starry crowd of heaven, we find new worlds revealed to us by every increase in the power of the telescope, than when the microscope discloses to us in a drop of water, or an atom of dust, new worlds of life and animation, or the remains of such as have passed away.

Whilst the tendency to push systematic investigation in every direction enables the individual mind of man to bring all the power of which he is capable to bear on the specialities of his study, and enables a greater number of labourers to take part in the universal work, it may be feared that that consciousness of its unity which must pervade the whole of Science, if it is not to lose its last and highest point of sight, may suffer. It has occasionally been given to rare intellects and the highest genius, to follow the various sciences in their divergent roads, and yet to preserve that point of sight from which alone their totality can be contemplated and directed. Yet how rare is the appearance of such gifted intellects ! and if they be found at intervals, they remain still single individuals, with all the imperfections of human nature.

The only mode of supplying with any certainty this want, is to be sought in the combination of men of science representing all the specialities, and working together for the common object of preserving that unity and presiding over that general direction.   This has been to some extent done in many countries by the establishment of Academies embracing the whole range of the Sciences, whether physical or metaphysical, historical or political.

FREEDOM OF HUMAN WILL.

WE hear it said, the prosecution of statistical inquiry leads necessarily to Pantheism and the destruction of true religion, as it deprives, in man's estimation, the Almighty of His power of free self-determination, making His world a mere machine, working according to a general pre-arranged scheme, the parts of which are capable of mathematical measurement, and the scheme itself of numerical expression; that it leads to fatalism, and therefore deprives man of his dignity, of his virtue and morality, as it would prove him to be a mere wheel in this machine, incapable of exercising a free choice of action, but predestined to fulfil a given task and to run a prescribed course, whether for good or for evil.

These are grave accusations, and would be terrible indeed if they were true. But are they true? Is the power of God destroyed or diminished by the discovery of the fact that the earth requires 365 revolutions upon its own axis to every revolution round the sun, giving us so many days to our year, and that the moon changes thirteen times during that period; that the tide changes every six hours; that water boils at a temperature of 212 degrees Fahrenheit; that the nightingale sings only in April and May; that all birds lay eggs; that 105 boys are born to every 100 girls? Or is man a less free agent because it has been ascertained that a generation lasts about forty years; that there are annually put in at the post-office the same number of letters on which the writers had forgotten to place any address; that the number of crimes committed under the same local, national, and social conditions is constant; that the full-grown man ceases to find amusement in the sports of the child?

ON THE ART-TREASURES EXHIBITION.

THE building in which we are assembled, and the wonderful collection of those treasures of art, as you so justly term them, which it displays, reflect the highest credit upon you. They must strike the beholder with grateful admiration, not only of the wealth and spirit of enterprise of this country, but also of that generous feeling of mutual confidence and goodwill between the different classes of society within it, of which it affords so gratifying a proof.

We behold a feast which the rich, and they who have, set before those to whom fortune has denied the higher luxuries of life—bringing forth from the innermost recesses of their private dwellings, and entrusting to your care, their choicest and most cherished treasures, in order to gratify the nation at large : and this, too, unhesitatingly, at your mere request, satisfied that your plans were disinterested and well matured, and that they had the good of the country for their object.

This is a gratifying sight, and blessed is the country in which it is witnessed. But not less so is the fact, which has shown itself in this as in other instances, that the great and noble of the land look to their Sovereign to head and lead them in such patriotic undertakings; and when they see that the Sovereign has come forward to give her countenance and assistance to the work, that they feel it a pleasure to co-operate with her and not to leave her without their support—emulating thus, in works of peace, the chivalric spirit which animated their forefathers in the warlike times of old.

You have done well not to aim at a mere accumulation of works of art, and objects of general interest, but to give to your collection, by a scientific and historical arrangement, an educational character—thus not losing the opportunity of teaching the mind, as well as gratifying the senses. And manifold are the lessons which it will present to us! If art is the purest expression of the state of mental and religious culture, and of general civilization of any age or people, an historical and chronological review given at one glance, cannot fail to impress us with a just appreciation of the peculiar characteristics of the different periods and countries the works of which are here exhibited to us, and of the influence which they have exercised upon each other.

In comparing these works with those of our own age and country, while we may well be proud of the immense development of knowledge and power of production which we possess, we have reason also for humility in contemplating the refinement of feeling and intensity of thought manifested in the works of the older schools.

THE INDIVIDUAL AND THE MASS.

STATISTICS are declared useless, because they cannot be relied on for the determination of any given cause, and do only establish probabilities where man requires and asks for certainty. This objection is well founded, but it does not affect the science itself, but solely the use which man has in vain tried to make of it, and for which it is not intended. It is the essence of statistical science that it only makes apparent general laws, but these laws are inapplicable to any special case; that, therefore, which is proved to be the law in general is uncertain in the particular. Thus are the power, wisdom, and goodness of the Creator manifested, showing how the Almighty has established the physical and moral world on unchangeable laws conformable to His eternal nature, while He has allowed to the individual the freest and fullest use of his faculties, vindicating at the same time the majesty of His laws by their remaining unaffected by individual self-determination.

PROFESSOR QUÉTÉLET.

I AM almost ashamed to speak such homely truths (of which I feel myself at best to be a very inadequate exponent) to a meeting like this, including men of such eminence in the science, and particularly in the presence of one who was your first President, M. Quétélet, and from whom I had the privilege, now twenty-four years ago, to receive my first instruction in the higher branches of mathematics—one who has so successfully directed his great abilities to the application of the science to those social phenomena, the discovery of the governing laws of which can only be approached by the accumulation and reduction of statistical facts.

SCIENCE AND THE BEGGING-BOX.

WE may be justified in hoping that, by the gradual diffusion of Science, and its increasing recognition as a principal part of our national education, the public in general, no less than the Legislature and the State, will more and more recognise the claims of Science to their attention; so that it may no longer require the begging-box, but speak to the State, like a favoured child to its parent, sure of his parental solicitude for its welfare; that the State will recognise in Science one of its elements of strength and prosperity, to foster which the clearest dictates of self-interest demand.

DR. JENNER.

THE discovery of vaccination was not the result of mere accident, like many other discoveries; but it was the result of long and thoughtful observation and reflection to which the discoverer's whole life was devoted. This country might be justly proud to number among her sons such a man as Jenner, for no man had been able to save so many lives as he had been able to do. His contemporaries had testified their approbation and feeling of gratitude for the important public service he had rendered; but it was reserved for our own day to inaugurate a memorial as a mark of our appreciation of Jenner's services in the cause of humanity. I hope that statue will be long preserved, to give the features of this benefactor of the human race for the contemplation and admiration of generations to come. I hope that vaccination will be further spread, for it is deplorable to think that, through neglecting it, fifty thousand victims still die annually in this country.

INDEX.

INDEX.

K

R. Clay, Son, & Taylor, Printers.

CPSIA information can be obtained
at www.ICGtesting.com
Printed in the USA
BVHW08s0847060818
523682BV00022B/1019/P